PRAGUE TR..... __

GUIDE 2023

70+ Ultimate Prague Experiences (With Pictures), Your Guide to All You Need to Know, where to Go, what to Do and Local Tips.

ADVENTURE PLANET

TABLE OF CONTENTS

PRAGUE IMAGES

MY EXPERIENCE

I moved to Prague a few years ago, after spending some time traveling around Europe. I was immediately taken with the city – its cobblestone streets, stunning architecture, and vibrant culture. I quickly fell in love with Prague and its people.

I had visited Prague as a tourist before, but living in the city gave me a different perspective. I explored the city in a way that I hadn't before, from the bustling streets of the Old Town to the tranquil gardens of the Prague Castle. I had the opportunity to experience the city from a unique point of view, and I knew immediately that I wanted to share this experience with others.

That's why I decided to write a travel guide about Prague. I wanted to help visitors get the most out of their trip to the city, show them the hidden gems that I had discovered, and give them an insight into the culture and people of Prague.

My travel guide includes all the must-see sights, from the Charles Bridge to the Astronomical Clock, and it also gives readers a glimpse into the everyday life in Prague, from the local pubs to basic Czech phrases. It's the perfect guide for anyone looking to explore the best of what Prague has to offer.

-Bianca.

ABOUT PRAGUE

The old-world beauty and charm of Prague makes it stand out among other cities in Europe. This vibrant Czech capital has a unique charm that radiates beyond its picturesque cobblestone streets and winding river. Its bridges, spires, and hilltop castles exude a captivating allure, often enhanced by the surprise of discovering a garden in the city's secluded courtyards. Not to mention its flourishing art scene and renowned entertainment.

In the past, its impeccably preserved Old City seemed to appear suddenly on the map for travellers, despite its medieval lanes and squares surviving the wartime bombings. Nowadays, it is a sought-after destination in Europe, although the winter has its own magic with its snow-capped roofs and icicle-laden churches, drawing fewer visitors.

The city's past has seen royal upheavals, renaissance movements, Nazi occupation and Soviet control, leaving behind a wealth of heritage for buffs to explore. Some of the classic sights include the Charles Bridge with its statues and the grand Prague Castle. Visitors can also explore the city's alleyways in search of chapels, courtyards and traditional Czech pubs with excellent beers.

The UNESCO-listed historic centre has more to offer with its luxury hotels, modern dining, shopping and entertainment. There are galleries, museums and clubs, with food and drink taken seriously here and nightlife far beyond the usual stag-do clichés.

The Czech capital is a city that can easily steal your heart. There is delicious and traditional cuisine to discover, a mix of architecture from Gothic to Cubism, and bold and humorous works of art to admire. Prague is somewhere to enjoy and appreciate.

PRAGUE'S HISTORY

The city's history dates back to the Celtic Boii tribe, who founded it around 500BC, and it wasn't until the German Marcomanni came along in AD9 that the tribe was displaced.

The Marcomanni were the progenitors of the Přemyslid dynasty, which reigned in Prague until the fourteenth century. Notable amongst the Přemyslid rulers was Wenceslas; he of Christmas carol fame, who was slain by his brother, Boleslav and was interred beneath St. Vitus's Cathedral. Despite recurrent political upheaval, the city prospered and became a major trading hub.

The true golden age of Prague began when Charles IV of Bohemia was elected as Holy Roman Emperor in the mid-fourteenth century. Imbued with fresh funds, Charles initiated a monumental building programme, including St. Vitus Cathedral and the Charles Bridge. Unfortunately, the legacy of Charles IV was squandered away by his irresponsible successors and when the last direct heir died without issue, Frederick V of Pfalz was elected king. His Calvinist faith, however, incurred the wrath of the Hapsburgs, and Catholic forces came out to vanquish him in 1620, leaving the Emperor Ferdinand II in control. With the political power now in Vienna, Prague slowly began to decline.

In the twentieth century, Prague was first subjected to Nazi occupation and then to the oppressive Soviet Union. Any opposition to the Soviet rule was met with harsh repression, most notably during the Prague Spring of 1968. Despite the trials and tribulations, the Czech spirit endured, and when the Berlin Wall fell in 1989, the people took the opportunity to break free from Communism in what was known as the Velvet Revolution. Subsequently, the Czechs and Slovaks divided, leaving Prague as the capital of the newly-established Czech Republic.

Are you aware that:

• Prague was the first Eastern Bloc city to be home to a Michelin-starred restaurant – the Allegro at the Four Seasons Hotel, which has since closed.

• It was in the Czech capital in 2006 that Pluto was demoted from a planet to a dwarf planet.

• The tomb of authoritarian Communist president Antonín Novotný does not have his name on it – the only hint of his existence is a personalized engraving.

PRAGUE'S WEATHER

Visiting Prague any time of year is a rewarding experience. During the spring **(March to May),** temperatures begin at 4°C (39°F) and rise to 15°C (59°F) by May, which is also when the city celebrates the Prague Spring International Music Festival and the Czech Beer Festival.

Summer **(June to August)** is quite pleasant in Prague and is overrun with tourists in July and August, although you should pack an umbrella in case of rain.

Autumn **(September to November)** is also lovely in Prague with low precipitation levels and temperatures that range from 14°C (57°F) in September to 3°C (37°F) in November.

During the winter months **(December to February),** Prague is known for its extended period of cold weather; however, the lack of tourists provides a peacefulness that enhances the beauty of the city's snow-covered bridges and castles. For an enchanting wintry scene, December and January are the best months to visit Prague and have the possibility of seeing a light coating of snow.

VISA AND PASSPORT REQUIREMENTS FOR CZECH REPUBLIC

	Passport Required	Return Ticket Required	Visa Required
USA	Yes	Yes	No
British	Yes	Yes	No
Canadian	Yes	Yes	No
Australian	Yes	Yes	No
EU	*See below*	No	No

Passports

EU Nationals: When travelling from one border-free Schengen country to another via car, it is not necessary to show a passport or national ID card. However, air, train and ferry companies will require you to display your passport or ID card to demonstrate your identity.

Non-EU Nationals: To enter Czechia, a valid passport issued in the last 10 years with a minimum of three months' validity remaining after the intended date of departure from the Czech Republic, along with a return ticket and sufficient funds for the duration of the stay, must be presented.

Czechia is included in the Schengen region, but be mindful that EU citizens such as Bulgaria, Cyprus, Ireland and Romania are not included, thus a passport or ID card is necessary if travelling to/from these countries.

Visas

EU Nationals: No visa is required for Czechia. Nevertheless, EU citizens intending to stay in Czechia for over 90 days must register with the local authorities before the expiration of the first 90 days.

Non-EU Nationals: Citizens of Non-EU countries and territories should check if they are allowed to visit Czechia and other Schengen countries.

For Hong Kong and Macao, holders of SAR passports do not require a visa for entry into Czechia.

Taiwan passport holders with identity card numbers are also exempt from needing a visa to enter the country.

Citizens of Serbia with biometric passports, excluding those issued by the Serbian Coordination Directorate, are also not required to obtain a visa.

Vanuatu: People holding passports issued on or after 25 May 2015 are not required to have a visa if they are from Vanuatu.

Additionally, nationals from the micro-states of Andorra, Monaco, San Marino and Vatican City do not need a visa.

Those from other countries should contact the nearest embassy to check visa requirements.

Visa Note

All travelers who do not currently require a visa to enter the Schengen nations must submit an ETIAS travel authorization application starting from November 2023.

Types and Cost

- The Schengen visa fee is €80 for those above 12 years old, €40 for children aged 6-12, and free for children below six.
- Nationals from Armenia, Russia and Azerbaijan pay €35.
- The visa fee is waived for certain applicants such as;
  i. School pupils, students, postgraduate students, and accompanying teachers on a study or educational trip
  ii. Researchers from third countries traveling to conduct scientific research

iii. Representatives of non-profit organizations aged 25 or less attending seminars, conferences, sports, cultural or educational events organised by non-profit organisations

iv. Family members of EU/EEA citizens.

Validity

The visa is valid for up to 90 days in any 180-day period.

Transit

Citizens of some countries need an airport transit visa when transiting through international parts of any airports within the Schengen countries, while citizens of certain countries may only require a transit visa for some of the Schengen countries. Those who are not from a Schengen visa-exempt country should check the requirements with a Czechia consulate nearby.

Application to

Get in contact with the relevant embassy, consulate or high commission.

Schengen Visas

It is necessary to note that Czechia is a Schengen country and the Schengen visa scheme applies.

Temporary Residence

For EU nationals, a long-term residence permit is required for stays of more than 90 days, while for non-EU nationals, a visa is necessary for stays of more than 90 days.

Working Days

It is important to be aware that Schengen visa applications usually take 15 calendar days, but can take up to 45 days, and it is recommended to submit applications four weeks prior to departure.

Proof of Funds

Applicants must provide proof of sufficient funds to cover their stay in the Czech Republic.

Compulsory Registration

Visitors who do not have a residence permit must register their accommodation address with the nearest foreign police department within 3 working days. EU nationals must do so within 30 days.

Extended Stay

Only in extraordinary situations may holders of Schengen visas who have visas that are less than 90 days' old extend their visas.

Entry with Pets

When bringing a pet from another EU country, the animal must have a microchip or tattoo, an EU pet passport, and a valid rabies vaccination certificate (vaccination must have taken place at least

21 days prior to travel). Animals coming from countries other than the EU must also have a 15-digit microchip that complies with ISO 11784/11785. Depending on whether the pet is from a high-rabies or a rabies-controlled country, the pet must either be vaccinated first or microchipped first. Additionally, a veterinary certificate issued by an authorised veterinarian is necessary when entering the Czech Republic with a pet from outside of the EU.

It is recommended to check with the relevant consulate for the appropriate procedures and to verify critical information with the embassy before travelling.

MONEY AND DUTY-FREE IN CZECH REPUBLIC

Currency

The official currency of the Czech Republic is the Koruna (CZK; symbol Kč) or Crown, which is equal to 100 haler. Notes are available in denominations of 5,000, 2,000, 1,000, 500, 200 and 100Kč, and coins can be found in 50, 20, 10, 5, 2 and 1Kč, and 50 haler.

Credit Cards

Most major credit cards such as American Express, Diners Club, Discover, Visa, and MasterCard are accepted for most transactions, although for smaller amounts cash might be necessary.

ATM

ATMs can be found across the country and usually offer an English translation.

Travellers Cheques

Traveller's cheques are accepted in banks but rarely in hotels and restaurants, and it is recommended to take them in US Dollars, Euros or Pounds Sterling to avoid additional exchange rate charges.

Banking Hours

Banking hours are typically from 9am to 5pm Monday to Friday, although some may close earlier on Fridays.

Currency Restrictions

There are no restrictions on the import or export of local or foreign currency; however, those travelling to or from a country outside the European Union must declare amounts over €10,000 or equivalent.

Currency Exchange

Foreign currency (including traveller's cheques) can be exchanged at banks, authorised exchange offices, main hotels and road border crossings.

Czech Republic Duty-Free

Overview

The Czech Republic is within the European Union and thus, travellers coming from outside the EU are entitled to buy certain items such as fragrance, cosmetics, skincare, champagne, selected spirits, wine, fashion accessories, souvenirs and gifts, all at tax-free equivalent prices.

For those travelling within the EU, if over 17 years old, you are free to buy and take goods with you, provided you have paid tax on them and they are for your own use (not for sale). However, if you bring in more than the following, customs officials may question you;

• One kg of tobacco, 800 cigarettes, 200 cigars or 400 cigarillos

• 90 liters of still wine, of which a maximum of 60 liters can be sparkling wine

• 110 liters of beer

• 10 liters of alcoholic beverages stronger than 22%, or 20 liters of fortified or sparkling wine or other liqueurs up to 22%.

However, travelers under 17 years old should check with applicable customs regulations prior to travelling.

For those coming from non-EU countries, a minimum age of 17 years is required to bring the following goods without incurring customs duty:

- 200 cigarettes or 100 cigarillos (max. 3 grams each) or 50 cigars or 250 grams of tobacco
- 4 liters of wine, 16 liters of beer, 1 liter of spirits over 22% volume, or 2 liters of alcoholic beverages less than 22%.
- For travellers arriving by car, petrol allowance is limited to one full tank plus an additional 10 liters in a portable container
- Other goods up to €430 for air and sea travellers, or €300 for other travellers (reduced to €200 for children under 15).

Banned Imports

Imports that are prohibited include explosives, addictive substances and any kind of waste. Firearms and ammunition are only allowed with a valid licence.

Restricted imports include animals, plants and food products. Non-EU travellers should not bring meat, dairy products, plants or cultural goods unless they have the correct certificates.

Banned Exports

Prohibited or restricted exports include veterinary goods, items of cultural value, weapons, ammunition, explosives and narcotics.

EASY WAYS TO AVOID ANNOYING THE LOCALS: A BRIEF GUIDE OF DO'S AND DONT'S

Gaining insight into the etiquette of Prague is essential when visiting the city. Czechs can be easily irritated by seemingly obvious, albeit stupid, circumstances, as well as surprisingly trivial details. As a Czech myself, I'd like to share some tips on how to avoid irritating the locals. Czechs are usually quite laid-back and there won't be any physical or verbal insults.

1. When Using Escalators, Make Sure to Stand On the Right Side.

This is the slower lane and is used primarily for those who want to ascend or descend the stairs. During peak hours it is not uncommon for people to stand on both sides, but it is still considered inappropriate.

Irritation level: 80%

2. Lower The Noise.

Czechs are very sensitive to noise and extravagant behaviour in public areas, such as restaurants, shops and tourist attractions. Loud conversations, whistling and chewing gum bubbles indoors are considered impolite. When getting on public transport, allow everyone to get off first before getting on.

Irritation level: 80%

3.   Refrain from Calling the Country "Eastern Europe".

It has been almost 35 years since the regime changed and Czech Republic is geographically located in the middle of Europe. The term "Central Europe" is much more appropriate.

Irritation level: 70%

4.   Prague Is Not a Playground for Adults.

Many tourists come to Prague for its nightlife and affordable alcohol, but they should remember that people still live and work in the city. Wearing bright costumes is fine, but vomiting or peeing in public, climbing statues or riding scooters while drunk is not.

Irritation level: 100%

5.   Follow The Rules in Churches, Historical Buildings and Concert Venues.

In churches, museums, and other historical buildings, it is considered discourteous to wear hats and sunglasses. It is recommended that you take off your cap when entering such places. When attending a concert, ballet, or opera, it is advisable to dress up smartly (although smart casual is typically acceptable, jeans, t-shirts, and sneakers are not).

Irritation level: 60 %

6.   Extend The Courtesy of Your Seat.

Offering one's seat to women, elderly, disabled, pregnant, or very small children is always appreciated. It is unpleasant to see all men seated while women have to stand. Very small children should be seated for their safety.

Irritation level: 70 %

7.   Please Do Not Leave Love Locks Here.

They will be disposed of in a scrap metal yard. This is not romantic and causes damage to railings, banisters, lamp posts, and fences due to the padlocks. Additionally, many keys are being thrown into rivers and cause rusting.

Irritation level: 70 %

8.   Do Not Drink or Eat Your Own Food in Cafés or Beer Gardens.

It is alright to consume food and drinks elsewhere, but it is considered inappropriate to do so in these places, as it harms the business.

Irritation level: 80 %

9.   "Historical" Cars.

"Historical" cars are actually replicas made a few years ago in Poland. Locals do not enjoy these cars as they take up a lot of space and worsen traffic. Tourists may enjoy these cars, but the locals roll their eyes.

Irritation level: 60 %

10.   Do Not Be Afraid to Drink Tap Water as It Is Safe Here.

It is recommended to bring a reusable bottle and refill it when necessary. Drinking fountains often provide cold tap water free of charge during the spring, summer, and autumn. Avoid buying plastic bottles if possible, as well as wasting food. It is disheartening to see tourists dumping food, causing bins in downtown areas to overflow with chimney cakes, sausages, unfinished coffee, unfinished beer, and bread.

Irritation level: 70%

And that's the end of it; Czechs are a fun-loving bunch (especially once they've had a beer), though they may be a bit on the conservative side.

YOUR PACKING CHECKLIST FOR YOUR PRAGUE VACATION

I t is no secret that we love traveling, however, packing for a trip isn't always an enjoyable process. Without a packing list, it can be difficult to remember all of the things we need to bring and it can sometimes lead to frustration. Thankfully, we can avoid this by following a few easy steps! Having a packing list not only helps us remember important items, but it also helps speed up the packing process.

This is why we have created a packing list specifically for Prague and the Czech Republic. This list contains all of the items we brought ourselves when we moved to Prague, and you can pick and choose what you need. Additionally, if you have any other items you need to bring (gifts, extra documents, medicine, etc.), you can add these to your note section to make sure they don't get left behind!

What Should You Purchase for Your Trip to Prague?

1.   Universal Adapter: As the majority of outlets in the Czech Republic are the same as the rest of the countries in the EU, you may want to bring a universal adapter to make sure you can use your devices no matter where you go. This eliminates the need to bring multiple adapters, which can take up a lot of space and can often get lost.

2.   Power Bank: Having a power bank with you is always a good idea, especially if you plan on doing some day trips from Prague and being on the go. It can be useful when your phone battery gets low, or you need to recharge your camera. In the Czech Republic, it is common to buy train tickets on your phone, so if your battery dies, you may get fined for not being able to show your ticket.

3.   Kindle: Reading a good book is a great way to relax during your travels. While physical books are great, they can take up a lot of space in your bag. Bringing a Kindle is a great alternative, as it is lightweight and can store a lot of books.

4.   Camera: No surprise here! We always bring a camera with us on our travels so that we can capture and look back on memories.

5.   Water Bottle: Having a water bottle with you is not only convenient but also environmentally friendly. Buying plastic water bottles adds up quickly and is bad for the environment, so it is nice to be able to fill up your own bottle wherever you go. The water in the Czech Republic is safe to drink.

6. **Sunscreen:** As the Czech Republic can get quite hot, it is important to bring sunscreen with you to protect your skin from sunburn.

7. **Sunglasses:** Sunglasses are a must-have when travelling, especially during the warmer months. The Czech Republic is quite sunny, so you will definitely get good use out of your sunglasses!

8. **Travel Insurance:** Last but not least, travel insurance is an essential item to bring. It can be a lifesaver in the event of an unexpected situation. Even though you may not expect anything bad to happen, it is always good to be prepared.

<u>Checklist for Prague: Essential Supplies</u>

Travel Necessities:

- Wallet
- Passport
- Travel insurance
- Driver's license
- Visa or MasterCard
- Czech Korunas (it's cheaper to get the money from your bank before you go).
- All of your electronics; phones, cameras, gadgets, and chargers

Clothing and Shoes:

- Underwear
- Socks
- A few pairs of shorts (hiking, runners, casual)
- Shirts for casual, dress, and sports (few of each)
- 2 or 3 pairs of pants
- Sneakers and sandals
- 1 sweater

Other items to bring:

- Day bag
- Toothbrush
- Hairbrush
- Toothpaste
- Floss
- Body lotions
- Extra toiletries
- Hand sanitizer
- Face masks

This packing list is useful for any European capital, making it easier to plan a trip and stay organized. Plus, it allows you to check items off as you go.

FAQ's

What Clothes Should I Bring to Prague?

Since Prague is in the middle of Europe, the weather can be quite hot in the summer and cold in the winter, so it's best to pack a combination of comfortable walking clothes as well as more formal attire for dinner and nightlife.

Is English Spoken in Prague?

Yes, most young people in the Czech Republic are proficient in English, and it's especially common in Prague. You should be able to get around and communicate in English when travelling to other cities, like Cesky Krumlov, Brno, or Pilsen.

Is Tipping Customary in Prague?

Tipping is common in Prague and it's not much different than in the UK or US. A 10-15% tip is usually given when the customer service is good. Keep in mind that the wages of the staff in restaurants and other places are not very high, so tipping helps them out.

Have a great time!

NAVIGATING PRAGUE: A COMPREHENSIVE GUIDE TO PUBLIC TRANSPORTATION

Navigating Prague is made easy by its world-class public transport system, which we will cover in this chapter. We will explain how to travel between the city's top attractions by metro, bus, tram, train, boat, or funicular and where to buy tickets.

Have you ever experienced a situation when something you had taken for granted your entire life did not meet your standards when you travelled abroad? This happened to us frequently over the past two years.

Having lived in Prague, we grew accustomed to the fact that its public transport is reliable and cheap. Buses, trams, metro, trains, and even boat transport are usually on time and the system is integrated, making it simple to use.

All we need to do is board the first available transport going in our direction. This is why Czechs living in Prague get frustrated when travelling abroad and the public transport does not live up to our expectations.

But even with an efficient and easy-to-use system, it can still be difficult to find your way around a strange city, especially if you are on a tight schedule, don't have a lot of time, don't speak Czech, and want to get from one point to the next quickly and without hassle.

In other words, when visiting Prague, you don't want to spend time studying the local transport, you just want to use it without having to think about it. Here, we will provide tips and tricks on how to navigate by metro, bus, tram, boat, or funicular.

TICKETS FOR PRAGUE'S PUBLIC TRANSPORTATION SYSTEM

Navigating Prague by public transport is inexpensive, even if you don't have an annual pass like we do. Nevertheless, if you are intending to stay in Prague for a longer time, you may want to consider investing in a top-up card called Litacka, but only if you are staying for over a month.

If you are visiting Prague for a regular trip, you are likely to purchase a normal paper ticket, which must be validated before you board public transport.

Remember to validate your paper ticket using the yellow validators or you will be fined by a controller even if you have a ticket. If you are caught without a valid ticket, the penalty can be very costly at a minimum of 1500 CZK.

In Prague, there are numerous ticket options. The great thing is that you can use the same ticket for the metro, tram, bus, boat, or even the funicular to Petrin Hill.

The cost of tickets varies depending on how long you plan to use public transport.

- A 30-MINUTE TICKET, which is 30 CZK (more than 1 EUR), allows you to use Prague transportation for 30 minutes.
- The 90-MINUTE TICKET, costing 40 CZK (less than 2 EUR), permits you to use transport for 90 minutes. Additionally, there are two multi-day plans.
- The 24-HOUR TICKET is 120 CZK and is valid for 24 hours from the time you validate the ticket.
- A 72-HOUR TICKET can be bought for 330 CZK, allowing you to use public transport for 3 days from the time you validate the ticket.
- If you plan on traveling with a dog or large luggage (more than 25cm x 45cm x 70cm), you should buy an additional ticket for 20 CZK. However, this extra charge does not apply if you've purchased a one-day or three-day ticket.

You can buy tickets at the metro vestibules.

How and Where Can I Buy Bus, Tram, And Metro Tickets In Prague?

There are several options for purchasing a ticket to get around Prague.

Ticket Machine

The yellow/orange vending machines found inside metro vestibules, tourist information centers, at bus or tram stops, tobacco shops, or serviced ticket booths in the subway are the most common places to buy tickets for Prague Public Transportation. Remember, that not all bus and tram stops feature vending machines, and drivers cannot sell tickets. Additionally, some vending machines only accept coins, while newer ones may accept credit cards.

On Board Ticket Machine

Inside the trams and some buses, you can use the ON BOARD TICKET MACHINE to pay with a contactless credit card and the ticket you purchase this way does not need to be validated. However, not all buses offer this service, so you will not know if the bus has a terminal until it arrives and you see the sign on the door.

SMS

Last but not least, you may purchase tickets for Prague Public Transport via SMS. To do this, you need a local SIM card with either a plan or credit and send a text message DPT31 or DPT42 (depending on the ticket you want to buy), on phone number 90206. The ticket will arrive within a minute, but you should not enter the vehicle until you receive confirmation of your payment.

MEANS OF TRANSPORTATION IN PRAGUE

Navigating public transport in Prague is straightforward as its system is not complicated. When visiting the capital of the Czech Republic for a couple of days, there are several ways to travel around the city;

METRO

The busiest means of transport is the metro. It is estimated that over one million people use the metro in Prague daily, making it one of the most heavily used undergrounds in the world. The metro system is easy to use and will take you to both the city center and the suburbs. In Prague, metro is the same as a subway.

Currently, there are only three lines in Prague - A (green line), B (yellow line) and C (red line). You can switch between the lines at Florenc, Muzeum, and Mustek. Also, each metro vestibule and platform has an easy-to-read map, with your current station encircled. You will be able to identify the next stop to the left or right of the map.

At peak times, the interval between trains is usually two minutes, usually early in the morning and later in the afternoon when people are commuting to and from work. During off-peak times, the interval is four to six minutes. The metro is the least likely to be delayed, so it is the best option if you are short on time. The subway is closed between midnight (or thirty minutes after midnight) and around 4:30 in the morning.

Without a doubt, the metro is the quickest way to get around Prague. However, if you only need to travel a few stops within the city center, it is not worth the effort to go underground. Instead, it is better to take a tram.

TRAM

The tram network within Prague city center is great, and it is the best way to sightsee as you travel between the main attractions. It is our preferred way to get around Prague, as we live in the city center and use it daily.

The most popular trams for sightseeing are number 9 and 22, and they usually run frequently, with a four to ten minute interval. Additionally, there is a historical tram running between mid-April to mid-November on weekends and national holidays. To use this tram, you need to purchase a special ticket for 50 CZK.

BUS

Taking the bus in the city center is not very practical and not necessary for most tourists. Buses usually service the outskirts and districts leading outside of the city, and unfortunately, are not always reliable due to traffic or accidents.

Nevertheless, most of the time they run on schedule. Bus stops usually terminate near metro and tram stations.

TRAIN

Another transportation option is the train, which is integrated into the public transport system and accessible with the same ticket. This is not very well-known to most visitors, since they generally stay in the historical part of Prague.

It may not be necessary to use trains when staying in the city center, however, it is good to be aware that this alternative does exist. The closest train stations to the center are Masarykovo Nadrazi, Hlavni Nadrazi, Nadrazi Vrsovice and Smichovske Nadrazi. Look for S trains with the PID logo if looking for the integrated ones.

FERRY AND BOAT TOUR

Taking a boat tour is another, albeit not the most practical, way to experience the city. Small ferries connect both banks of the Vltava river and provide beautiful views. It is also a budget-friendly option to experience a boat ride without joining an expensive tour.

Our favorite line out of the seven is number P5, which runs between Cisarska Louka, Vyton and Naplavka Smichov. On a clear day, you can spot the Vysehrad and Prague Castle from this boat, which has a capacity of 12 people. Standard public transport tickets can be used for this service, however, it is important to check the timetable as ferries go every fifteen or thirty minutes and some lines don't run all year round.

FUNICULAR

Petrin Hill, located near Prague Castle, provides one of the best views of Prague. To reach the peak, you can either take a leisurely 25-minute walk or ride the funicular up.

The great thing about the Petrin funicular is that it is part of Prague's public transport system, so your 24-hour or 72-hour pass can be used. The downside is that this line is frequently visited by tourists, so you may have to wait in line for a while.

When the weather is nice, we prefer to take a stroll as there are multiple trails leading up to the Eiffel Tower of Prague.

ON FOOT

Prague is not as big as New York, and most of its famous attractions can be explored on foot. It's also not as dangerous as Rio de Janeiro, so you won't have to worry about your expensive camera or wallet.

We usually choose to walk in Prague when possible.

Did you know that you can reach the Old Town Square from Prague Castle in less than twenty minutes on foot? Or from National Theatre to Vysehrad in half an hour? It's a pleasant, peaceful and picturesque journey along Naplavka - Rasinovo Nabrezi, one of the liveliest places in Prague.

Plus, walking is free and good for your health.

CAR

Generally, we wouldn't suggest renting a car if your agenda only includes touring the city center of Prague. You'll be spending a lot of time looking for a parking space, and you could easily get lost in the narrow one-way streets.

On the other hand, if you plan on doing day trips from Prague, for example to Terezin or Ostrava, you may find a car rental useful.

Public Transport to The Best Attractions in Prague

Although we don't know which hotel in Prague you will stay, and in which area you will choose to reside, there are many lines you will likely find useful when navigating the city. Even though the city center of Prague is relatively small and one can walk to most places, you still need a starting point.

To reach Wenceslas Square and Vysehrad, take metro line C and disembark at Muzeum or Vysehrad station. Line A is useful to get to Prague Castle or Charles Bridge; take the green line to Malostranska or tram 22.

To get to Old Town Square or Republic Square, take the yellow line B and disembark at Namesti Republiky station. We prefer using trams in Prague as the system is widespread, but make sure it's suitable for you after you book your hotel.

Buses mainly traverse the outskirts, but they also run in the center; however, you are unlikely to need them.

What to Know About Public Transport in Prague

No matter if you are taking the metro, bus, or tram for the first time in Prague, there are some essential points to keep in mind.

SAFETY

Although Prague is generally considered to be a secure city, this does not mean that there aren't any people attempting to take advantage of tourists who are not being mindful and watching their belongings. When you're on the tram, bus, or metro, make sure you know where your items of value are, and never leave your bag unattended due to pickpockets, especially on key routes which take thousands of tourists to the must-see places in Prague (tram line number 22). We have never encountered an issue on public transport, but it is always better to be informed and vigilant than sorry.

MOBILE APP

Prior to using public transport in Prague, make sure to download the Jizdni Rady app. This app will make your travels around Prague much easier since you can always enter your location or the nearest station and the destination you want to get to, and the app will show you the best route, timetable, where to change lines if needed, the duration of the journey and the cost of the ticket required. We use this app daily, and it has never let us down. From time to time, certain lines may be rerouted due to construction work or an accident. If there are any long-term repairs, you will be able to find the updated schedule on the Jizdni Rady app. You will also be able to tell if a line has been rerouted when at the bus or tram station because the line number will be marked in yellow as opposed to white.

SERVICE DISRUPTIONS

In case of an accident, for example, when someone jumps under a train, there will always be an alternative transport beginning with the letter X. So if it is, for instance, not possible to proceed on your metro route C, go above ground and look for a bus XC.

DOORS

Doors on public transport do not usually open automatically, and you will need to press a button.

ALWAYS GIVE WAYS TO TRAMS

Never cross the street in front of a tram, it won't stop. Ever. Make sure to always give way to trams in Prague.

How to Get Around Prague at Night

If you are planning on going to the theatre, cinema, or bar and know you will be out late at night, you don't have to rely on an expensive taxi to get back to your hotel. The regular Prague daytime service of metro, trams and buses typically run between 4:30 AM till midnight (0:30 AM).

After midnight, however, you can use night trams and buses which run regularly, every 30 minutes. Night buses use the numbers 901–915 and tram lines have the numbers 91–99. All night trams connect at Lazarska, where you can switch lines, and buses follow up on tram lines or other bus lines, so you will always be able to find a tram or bus to safely take you back to your hotel or hostel.

Frequently Used Forms of Tourist Transportation in Prague

Apart from walking, which is our favorite way of getting around the city centre, other new and modern forms of transport have been introduced in Prague, just like in other popular tourist spots in Europe.

Although we're not overly keen on bikes or scooters in the city centre, we can appreciate that they can be an enjoyable way to visit some of the must-see attractions, particularly for younger travellers or those who want to experience the city from a different angle.

When renting either a bike or scooter, it is essential to drive with care and not put other drivers or pedestrians at risk. There are plenty of places to rent either bike or scooter, and many tours available; we have selected some of the finest one's for you:

• Electric Bikes Prague Sightseeing Tour; for 3 hours of detailed e-bike exploration of the city's best viewpoints

• Prague Small-Group Segway Tour; to uncover less touristy sights in Prague with a local guide

• Private Electric Bike Prague Tour; with a local guide to reveal the most renowned sights in Prague like Prague Castle, Old Town or John Lennon Wall, with hotel pickup service

- E-Scooter Prague Tour; to observe the most significant historical places in Prague in just two hours
- Prague Beer Bike Tour; to pedal around the best sights in Prague while sipping premium Czech ice-cold beer. What an adventure!

How to Take Public Transport from Prague Airport to The City Center

If you're flying into Prague, you may be searching for how to get from the airport to the city's centre. For us, this is typically the most expensive and irritating part of getting around a city, something we're not fond of. Taking a taxi is an option in Prague, but due to the bad rep of the taxi drivers there, we suggest using an Uber instead. However, if you're trying to stay on a budget, public transport is the way to go. Purchase a ticket for 40 CZK, wait for bus number 119 in front of the terminal, and get off at Nadrazi Veleslavin, where you need to switch to the metro.

WHERE TO STAY IN PRAGUE FOR ALL BUDGET TYPES

L ocated in Central Europe, Prague- the capital of the Czech Republic - is a comparatively small city, yet it offers the unique advantage of being brimming with history and being navigable by foot. From the terraces and rooftop beer gardens, you can enjoy the beauty of the Old Town, which is a real melting pot of architectural styles.

Where Can I Stay in Prague?

It is not always easy to decide where the best place to stay in Prague is, but fret not! I have created this guide to help you make the perfect decision, so that you can have a stress-free holiday. It includes recommendations on where to stay in Prague, tailored to the needs of backpackers, first-time visitors and those travelling with children. So, without further ado, let's begin!

CHARMING FAMILY APARTMENT- BEST AIRBNB IN PRAGUE

The best Airbnb in Prague is the Charming Family Apartment, where up to seven guests can stay. It boasts a fully-equipped kitchen, soundproof windows and modern interior design with preserved wooden floors. The apartment is within walking distance of numerous attractions, such as the old town square, and it is located in one of the trendiest areas of the city.

ROADHOUSE PRAGUE- BEST HOSTEL IN PRAGUE

The Roadhouse Prague is the best hostel to stay in. It is a modern, award-winning hostel that opened in 2017 and has already won the hearts of many travellers. It is centrally located, close to many tourist attractions and the Vltava River. It offers bunk beds in shared dorms, with curtains for privacy, lockable storage space and individual power outlets.

HOTEL INOS- BEST BUDGET HOTEL IN PRAGUE

Hotel Inos is the best budget hotel in Prague. It provides spacious rooms located 10 minutes away from the Old Town by tram, and right on the Vltava River. Every room has a private bathroom, a flat-screen TV and free wifi, while some of them also have a balcony. A buffet breakfast with traditional Czech dishes is served to the guests every morning.

So, to sum up, Prague is a great destination for all types of travellers, as it is small, yet full of interesting sights to see. There are many distinct neighborhoods to stay in, and each one has a special charm. Whether you're a backpacker, a first-time visitor or travelling with kids, you will be close to all the main attractions, no matter where you choose to stay.

For those making their first trip to Prague, they will be delighted by the quaintness and central locale of Old Town, where a lot of tourists can be seen each day. This is where you can find the renowned Old Town Square, Wenceslas Square, Charles Bridge, and the Astronomical Clock, which is what most consider to be the core of Prague.

On the other side of the Vltava River, the Mala Strana, or Little Quarter, provides a more tranquil atmosphere and is suitable for those travelling with their families, who are seeking a calmer setting while still being close to the action. This area bears Prague Castle and the Charles Bridge.

Apart from the Old Town, the Prague New Town is more than 700 years old and located a bit further away from the main attractions. Due to this, it is a great option for those who are looking for a cheaper accommodation option, such as backpackers. There are numerous eateries and coffee shops in the vicinity.

Vinohrady has become the trendiest district of Prague, with its laid-back atmosphere and multiple dining options that will please the trendiest among us. In the summer, Havlickovy park serves as a great spot to bask in nature and escape from the hustle of the downtown area.

If you are looking to do some of the great day trips in Prague, make sure to stay in an area with convenient access to public transport.

Top Five Areas in Prague

Examining the top 5 spots to stay in Prague can help you decide which one is the most suitable for you.

OLD TOWN – WHERE TO STAY FOR FIRST-TIMERS

To begin with, Old Town is the most central district in the city and is a great option if it is your first time visiting. This section of the city is the most popular choice among tourists, as it has a lot of historic attractions and eateries. Additionally, the Charles Bridge and some luxury hotels are situated in the city centre.

It is also worth noting that the Astronomical Clock in Old Town Square is a renowned activity that many visitors come to experience. The square is a great place to sit and have a drink, a snack, or a hot chocolate during the winter. The Old Town Hall building can be visited, and the top of the tower offers a spectacular panoramic view of the city.

Exploring this area will give you the chance to witness some of Prague's finest architecture, some of which dates back to the 8th century.

Massive Old Town Apartment- Best Airbnb in Old Town

If you are looking for the best Airbnb in Old Town, then the Massive Old Town Apartment is the one you should go for. It has two bedrooms and more than enough room for up to six guests. Plus, it is just a few steps away from Old Town Square and Charles Bridge, with all the main attractions in the city. If you are looking for great value for your money, then this Airbnb is the one to choose!

Dream Hostel Prague- Best Hostel in Old Town

Dream Hostel Prague is an ideal place for backpackers in Prague. It is not only stylish, but also very reasonably priced. Furthermore, the staff are incredibly welcoming and helpful. You will get a lot of value for such a low price when staying at this hostel. Check out the photos and reviews and you won't be disappointed!

Old Prague Hotel- Best Budget Hotel in Old Town

The Old Prague Hotel is a great budget option if you are looking to stay in Old Town. It offers air conditioning, private bathrooms and flat-screen TVs in all its rooms. Plus, it has a free WiFi connection and a delicious breakfast buffet every morning.

Hotel Melantrich- Best Mid-Range Hotel in Old Town

Hotel Melantrich is a great mid-range accommodation option in Old Town. It has recently been renovated and offers air conditioning, private bathrooms and flat-screen TVs in all its rooms. Plus, it has free WiFi throughout the hotel and allows pets.

Sights and Activities to Explore in Old Town

• Gaze upon the cityscape from the summit of the Old Town Hall

• View the show at regular intervals on the astronomical clock

• Stroll the Royal Route just as the former Czech Kings did on the way to Prague Castle

- Relax in a café located in the Old Town Square

NEW TOWN - WHERE TO STAY ON A BUDGET IN PRAGUE

Located directly adjacent to Old Town, New Town may be termed as such, yet much of the area is actually about seven centuries old! Although it does not contain as many of Prague's primary attractions, there are still some wonderful sights to behold in this district. Foremost of these is the Dancing House, a structure created by Frank Gehry that takes inspiration from the renowned couple, Fred Astaire and Ginger Rogers.

Wenceslas Square is the principal square in New Town, where you can try the finest Czech cuisine and view some of the most phenomenal architecture. Lastly, if you have the opportunity, the National Theatre is a must-visit to enjoy a spellbinding cultural show.

Hostel One Home- Best Hostel in New Town

Hostel One Home is the ideal choice for those looking for a cozy home away from home in New Town. Backpackers will be delighted to find this is one of the best party hostels in Prague and provides the perfect opportunity to meet new people. Every night, the staff cooks a free dinner and takes guests to the local bars and pubs. The rooms offer dorm beds and free Wifi.

Wenceslas Square Hotel- Best Budget Hotel in New Town

The Wenceslas Square Hotel provides clean and comfortable rooms at an affordable price. Each room includes a private bathroom, a flat-screen TV, a fan and free Wifi access. During the summer months, guests can take advantage of the hotel garden. A bar and a restaurant offering brunch is also present there.

Hotel Majestic Plaza- Best Mid-Range Hotel in New Town

The Hotel Majestic Plaza is an elegant boutique hotel located within walking distance of Wenceslas Square and housed in two historic buildings. Rooms are equipped with air conditioning, a private bathroom, a flat-screen TV and a tea and coffee maker.

Chic Modern Home- Best Airbnb in New Town

Chic Modern Home is a great Airbnb option in New Town that offers modern interior design at a reasonable price. Guests can relax on the retro blue velvet couch and watch Netflix or Hulu on the flat-screen TV. The home is located in a historic building and is close to Wenceslas Square and a range of cafes. The neighbourhood is full of authentic and interesting pieces that make Prague such a great destination.

Sights and Activities to Explore in New Town

• Sampling the cuisine of the Czech Republic in Wenceslas Square

• Attending a performance at the National Theatre

• Be amazed by the eccentricity of the Cerny sculptures in Lucerna Passage and Narodni.

- Admiring the one-of-a-kind design of the Dancing House

ZIZKOV - WHERE TO STAY FOR NIGHTLIFE IN PRAGUE

Situated in a more remote area than the historical centre, Zizkov is a mainly residential area with a vibrant and alive Prague nightlife scene. Many travellers choose to stay in this neighbourhood due to the more affordable accommodation prices. There is great public transport links to the city centre, so it's easy to get there.

Although it was once a Communist stronghold, nowadays it is known as the neighbourhood with the most bars per capita in Europe, making it the perfect place to be if you're looking for a great nightlife experience. The most recognisable feature of Zizkov is the TV Tower, which was originally used to block signals from the West. Nowadays, the tower has a restaurant at its base, and visitors can take the elevator to the top to take in the breathtaking views of Prague.

Cozy and Chic Studio- Best Airbnb in Zizkov

The top Airbnb in Zizkov is the Cozy and Chic Studio, which is quite small but offers all the amenities you could need. From a TV and a fully-equipped kitchen to an incredible location near plenty of nightlife spots, this studio is sure to please nightlife aficionados. With a mix of hip, green, and authentic beauty, you'll feel right at home!

Clown and Bard- Best Hostel in Zizkov

The Clown and Bard hostel offers guests a variety of private rooms and dormitory accommodations. You'll have your own personal locker, as well as access to free WiFi.

Hotel Amadeus Prague- Best Budget Hotel in Zizkov

If you're looking for a budget-friendly option, Hotel Amadeus Prague is the perfect place for you. Each room is fitted with a private bathroom, a patio, and a seating area. The hotel is located in a peaceful area of the neighbourhood and a delicious breakfast is provided every morning. Plus, an airport shuttle service is available and it's just a few steps from the nearest metro station.

Carlton Hotel Prague- Best Mid-Range Hotel in Zizkov

For mid-range accommodation, be sure to check out the Carlton Hotel Prague. This newly-refurbished hotel offers modernly decorated rooms with private bathrooms, air conditioning, and flat-screen TVs. Non-smoking rooms are available, and guests will enjoy free WiFi access and a delicious buffet breakfast every morning. The front desk is open 24/7 and public transportation is easily accessible.

Sights and Activities to Explore in Zizkov

• Experience a stunning sunset at the Prague Castle from Riegrovy Sady, one of the city's most remarkable parks.

- Take in the impressive views of Prague from atop the Zizkov Television Tower.

- Behold the largest clock in the nation at the Church of the Most Sacred Heart of Our Lord.

- Unwind and have a great time in Zizkov's various pubs and beer gardens.

VINOHRADY - THE HIPPEST NEIGHBORHOOD IN PRAGUE

What was once a large vineyard in the 14th century has now become Prague's trendiest area. It is conveniently located a few stops away from the New Town and Old Town, and staying in Vinohrady will provide more tranquillity.

Havlickovy Sady, Prague's next biggest park, is located in Vinohrady and is a must-see. Take a stroll to admire the gorgeous Italian Renaissance-style villa and the vineyard, offering a reminder of Vinohrady's past. During WWII, it was used as a training centre for the Hitler Youths.

Peace Square is another must-visit area in Prague. It is relatively small and has a charming market that runs around the Christmas and Easter period. Whilst you're there, make sure to check out the Cathedral of St Ludmila, built in Gothic style in the 19th century.

Cozy and Modern Studio- Best Airbnb in Vinohrady

If you're looking for the ultimate accommodation experience in Vinohrady, then this cozy and modern studio is perfect for you! Located in one of the coolest areas in Prague, you'll be within easy walking distance of many of the city's monuments. Your host will provide a travel guide and detailed map of the neighbourhood, so you'll never get lost.

Arkada Hotel Praha- Best Budget Hotel in Vinohrady

For those on a budget, the Arkada Hotel Praha offers comfortable rooms with a private bathroom, a view of the city, and amenities such as a fan, heating, and a free Wifi connection.

Elizabeth Suites- Best Mid-Range Hotel in Vinohrady

If you're looking for something a bit more luxurious, then the Elizabeth Suites is the ideal mid-range hotel. It offers modernly decorated rooms with a seating area, kitchenette, private bathroom, and a flat-screen TV with satellite channels. Some rooms even have a terrace. This hotel also provides a free Wifi connection and airport shuttle service.

American Loft in The Heart of Prague- Another Great Airbnb Option in Vinohrady

For a truly unique experience, check out the American Loft in the Heart of Prague! This stylish loft features exposed brickwork, an indoor sauna (for an extra fee), and a special wine storage room. It's great for socializing, with enough space for up to 6 guests. You'll love the massive living room and kitchen area and the charming details throughout.

Sights and Activities to Explore in Vinohrady

• Take some time to unwind in Havlickovy Sady, Prague's second-largest park.

• Enjoy the stunning Art Deco houses that line the streets

• Treat yourself to one of the few street food options in the city, a hot dog from the Peace Square.

MALA STRANA - THE BEST PRAGUE NEIGHBORHOOD FOR FAMILIES

Situated on the opposite side of the water from Old Town, Mala Strana, otherwise known as Lesser Town, is a much quieter area that is still in the heart of Prague, allowing for easy access to all the main attractions. This makes it a perfect spot for a family to stay during a quick weekend in the city.

When one crosses Charles Bridge, which was constructed in the fourteenth century, they can take in the astonishing sights of the Vltava River with street performers and musicians all around. In Mala Strana, visitors have the privilege of exploring Prague Castle, the biggest castle complex on the planet, which was set up in 880. This castle is a UNESCO World Heritage site and is a major symbol of the Czech Republic.

Quite Stylish Old Town Apt near Charles Bridge- Best Airbnb in Mala Strana

One of the top Airbnbs in Mala Strana, Quite Stylish Old Town Apt near Charles Bridge. This home has huge windows that bring in natural light and can accommodate up to four people. It's also conveniently located within walking distance of the tram, so you can easily explore the city.

Charming Family Apartment- Another Great Airbnb option in Mala Strana

For a larger family, there's another great Airbnb in Mala Strana which is a cozy and vibrant apartment that sleeps up to seven guests. It has a fully equipped kitchen, comfortable mattresses, soundproof windows, and a modern interior with preserved wooden floors. Plus, the host provides a personalised guidebook with their local recommendations to enhance your stay.

Hotel U Schnellu- Best Budget Hotel in Mala Strana

For those looking for a budget-friendly option in Mala Strana, Hotel U Schnellu is a great choice. This family-run establishment offers cosy rooms with a private bathroom, air conditioning, and a flat-screen TV. Plus, you can enjoy views of Prague's stunning architecture from your room.

Hotel Pod Vezi- Best Mid-Range Hotel in Mala Strana

For those who want a bit more luxury, Hotel Pod Vezi is a great mid-range option. This hotel is located in a historical building right next to the iconic Charles Bridge. It provides rooms with an ensuite bathroom, air conditioning, soundproofing, and a flat-screen TV. There is also a bar and restaurant, plus a delicious breakfast served in the morning.

Sights and Activities to Explore in Mala Strana

• Explore the expansive Prague Castle, the largest coherent castle complex in the world

• Marvel at the views of the Vltava River from the fourteenth century Charles Bridge.

• Gain insight into the life and works of renowned Czech author Franz Kafka at the Franz Kafka Museum.

• Pay homage at the John Lennon Wall.

Our Concluding Remarks Regarding Accommodation in Prague....

Prague is a stunning city in Europe, boasting a plethora of historical structures and attractions. Moreover, it is one of the least expensive places to stay and dine in Europe, thus making it a must-visit if you are touring the continent. The Hotel Savoy, situated in the center of Prague, is my top recommendation for accommodations, as it provides excellent services at a remarkable cost.

For those travelling on a tight budget, The Roadhouse Prague is an excellent choice, as it opened in 2017 yet has already become one of the most sought-after locations in the city.

THE TOP 25 THINGS TO DO IN PRAGUE, CZECH REPUBLIC

This chapter will provide a comprehensive guide to the top offerings of the incredible city of Prague. The city has been around for over a millennium and is renowned for its exquisite beauty. Additionally, there is much more to see and do than just admiring its grandeur. With the Vltava River running through it, Prague is a masterpiece of Gothic and Renaissance architecture, museums, and churches.

Before your trip, it is wise to book some of the tours and activities online, take advantage of the Prague City Card for discounts and unlimited public transportation, and explore Prague in the day and evening. Moreover, you can enjoy Czech cuisine and the best lagers in the world. Activities such as jazz music, puppet shows, pork knuckles, and the astronomical clock are some of the things to do in Prague.

The Prague Card covers 2, 3, or 4 Days in Prague and provides free entrance to over 60 attractions. This includes a cruise on the Vltava River, a bus tour, and free entry to famous Prague attractions such as Prague Castle, St. Vitus Cathedral, Royal Palace, Golden Lane, St. George's Basilica, the Jewish Museum (including the synagogues and Old Jewish Cemetery), the National Gallery (7 sites), the National Museum (9 sites), Petrín View Tower and Petrín Mirror Maze, and much more.

1.   Take A Free Stroll Across the Charles Bridge

Take a free stroll across the Charles Bridge, constructed in 1357 by Charles IV, and completed in 1390. The statues along the bridge were added in the 17th century and the bridge was not given its name until the 19th century.

2.   Tour The Old Town Square

Tour the Old Town Square, which has been preserved since the 10th Century. It is a popular attraction with a variety of street performers, merchants, and restaurants that are sure to entertain. The architecture of the square is also worth admiring.

3.   Witness The Striking of the Hour at The Astronomical Clock

Witness the striking of the hour at the Astronomical Clock located on the south face of the Old Town Hall. Built in the 15th Century, it is the best preserved medieval mechanical clock in the world and the performance at the top of the hour is always a crowd pleaser.

4.   Visit The Infant Jesus of Prague

Visit the Infant Jesus of Prague in the Mala Strana area of the city, a Roman Catholic statue of Jesus Christ believed to be from the 16th Century. Hundreds of believers come to the shrine daily to pray, bow and make wishes that they hope will come true. It is encased in an ornate gilded shrine.

5.   Visit The Old Jewish Ghetto

Visit the old Jewish Ghetto, located between the Old Town and the Vltava River. Jews were ordered to settle in the area in the 13th century and were banned from living anywhere else in the city. Although many buildings were destroyed in the late 19th century, several significant historical buildings remain, including six synagogues.

6.   Discover The Fascinating KGB Museum

Discover the fascinating KGB Museum, founded by a Russian enthusiast and housing a variety of artifacts related to the Soviet Union's secret police. Inside, you can find spy cameras, secret weapons, interrogation equipment, and photographs of Prague taken in 1968 that show the city's streets eerily empty.

7.   Make A Pilgrimage to Prague Castle

Make a pilgrimage to Prague Castle, located in the district of Hradcany. This breath-taking fortress has been the seat of Czech leaders throughout history and the current home of the president. Visitors to the grounds of the castle can enter free of charge, although tickets are needed to enter the St Vitus Cathedral, Basillica of St George, and Golden Lane. If you're looking to avoid long queues, you can purchase Skip the Line: Prague Castle Tickets, or opt for the 2.5-Hour Tour (including admission ticket) for a guided experience.

8.   Explore The Treasures of St Vitus Cathedral

Explore the treasures of St Vitus Cathedral, a structure that appears to have been standing for centuries, but was in fact only completed in 1929. Visitors can take in the tomb of St John of Nepomunk, the Chapel of St Wenceslas, and the impressive art nouveau stained glass. Tours including admission tickets are available for the cathedral, such as the 2.5-Hour Prague Castle Tour.

9.   Step into The Mysterious Golden Lane

Step into the mysterious Golden Lane, a street rumored to be a playground for alchemists searching for a reaction to turn ordinary materials into gold, although the accuracy of this claim is debatable. Famous Czech-Jewish writer Franz Kafka lived in a house on the street for two years, finding solace in the peaceful atmosphere.

10.   Sample The Classic Czech Dish of Pork Knuckle

Sample the classic Czech dish of Pork Knuckle, also known as Koleno. This hunk of marinated pork knee is served with pickled vegetables and dark Czech bread, and is sure to draw attention as you tackle the large portion of meat.

11.   Explore The Statue of Sigmund Freud

Take a stroll through the stunning Old Town of Prague and you will be surprised to find a seven-foot-tall sculpture of the renowned psychoanalyst Sigmund Freud suspended from a metal beam above the cobblestone streets. The unusual artwork has been presented in various cities around the world, including Chicago, London, and

Berlin. It has even caused a few calls to the emergency services, as it has been mistaken for a suicide attempt.

12.   Pay Tribute to John Lennon

Though situated far away from Liverpool, the birthplace of the Beatles, fans should definitely make a pilgrimage to this homage to one of the most renowned bands ever. The wall has been decorated with John Lennon and The Beatles graffiti, lyrics, and quotes since the 1980s and is a popular destination for tourists and young admirers wishing to show their respect.

13.   Shop at The Farmer's Market

Found beneath the fortress of Vysehrad, foodies should consider visiting this farmer's market, which pops up every Saturday.

Mingle with the locals as you sample some of the finest food (and views) the city has to offer. From seasonal vegetables and freshly-baked bread to pickles, preserves, sausages, and other speciality meats, you can enjoy your purchases while sitting by the riverbank and observing the daily life of Prague.

14.   Watch A Puppet Performance

The citizens of Prague have a strong connection to puppetry. The city has more than 20 puppet shops, 30 puppeteers, and even a puppet museum. It is believed that puppetry has been popular in Prague since the 12th century, when the figurines were used for entertainment at royal feasts and ceremonies. For a puppet show, visitors should check out the National Marionette Theatre or Theatre Spejbla & Hurvinek for a memorable performance.

15.   Discover The History of Communism

Europe is a continent with a tumultuous past, and the Czech Republic is no exception. The nation was a communist state from 1948 until the overthrow of the regime in 1989. Over 200,000 people were detained and 327 killed while attempting to flee the country. The museum of communism features photographs, videos, and sculptures that document the state-sanctioned terrorism of the communist era.

16.   Sail Down the Vltava

Take a cruise on the river Vltava for an unparalleled view of the many historical landmarks and monuments. Voyages within the city are affordable and some even include a meal depending on the time of day. To be able to fully appreciate the tranquil banks, it is recommended to choose a cruise lasting at least two hours.

17.   Drink A Renowned Brew (Or Two)

Satisfy your curiosity for beer by drinking a renowned brew (or two) in Prague. It is said that the Czechs have the best beer in the world, and local bars can provide lagers like Budvar and Staropramen, as well as craft beers from the country's top microbreweries. Most Czech beers are light and brewed from hand-picked hops. Increasingly, dark ales are also available, but the Czechs prefer their beer light and chilled with a foam head. Beer lovers should visit the Prague Beer Museum to sample more than 31 quality beers on tap.

18.   Witness The Changing of the Guard at The Castle

Be sure to witness the Changing of the Guard at the castle. The ceremony includes a fanfare and flag ceremony, and the guards wear unique uniforms that are light blue in summer and dark blue in winter.

19.   Take A Leisurely Stroll Through Mala Strana

Take a leisurely stroll through the baroque alleyways of Mala Strana, the Lesser Quarter which was built in the 17th and 18th centuries by victorious Catholic clerics and noblemen on the ruins of their Protestant predecessors' Renaissance palaces. In the center of the district is a pleasant square featuring small shops to explore, traditional Czech pubs and restaurants, and stunning views of the river.

20.   Visit Letna Park and Watch the Skateboarders!

This old park was once home to a colossal statue of Joseph Stalin before it was demolished in the 1960s. It is now a popular gathering place for skateboarders, located on the inclined embankment of Letna Hill. Kick back and relax in one of the many beer gardens, and even if the skateboarders don't keep you occupied, the city's ever-changing skyline surely will.

21.   Experience The Vibrant Nightlife of Prague.

Known for its jazz and classical music, there are a plethora of live music venues in the city that can guarantee a good night out. JazzDock is a great spot to visit and features some of the city's best local jazz musicians. For clubbers, the Cross Club is an industrial-style nightclub with a unique interior filled with gadgets, cranks and shafts that move to the music.

22.   Indulge in The Pickled Cheese!

This Czech delicacy is a must-try for those with a love for food. A perfect accompaniment to a glass of cold pivo, this dish is an iconic Czech pub classic. Composed of a soft Camembert-type cheese, with an edible rind, pickled in oil, spices and garlic, it is served with chilli peppers and Czech fried bread. This snack is both creamy and blazingly hot, and is a great way to sample Czech cuisine. If you're after more, why not explore one of the city's Food Tours?

23.   Put Your Intellect to The Test at The Mind Maze!

This challenge, inspired by the legends of alchemists, is an unforgettable experience. When you enter the Mind Maze, you are locked in the Alchemist's chamber and must escape within an hour by solving a series of puzzles and riddles. At first, the chamber appears to be aged and sparsely populated, but when you take a closer look, you realise there is much more to this room than meets the eye. Bring a friend for a better chance of escape - two heads are always better than one!

24.   Spend Some Time in Nature at Jelení Príkop (Stag Moat)!

If the bustle of Prague has become too much, this hidden gem is the perfect spot for a break. Formerly a moat alongside Prague Castle, this stretch of greenery is now the ideal area to have a picnic or take a leisurely stroll before dinner. Take some time to relax here and recharge after all the exploring in Prague.

25.　Climb The 299 Steps of Petrin Hill

Climb the 299 steps of Petrin Hill for spectacular views of the city and to relax in its lush greenery. Alternatively, you can take the funicular railway to the summit to visit the miniature Eiffel Tower, landscaped gardens, and the Church of St. Michael, a wooden building originally from Ukraine.

NIGHTLIFE IN PRAGUE

B efore anything else, Prague provides a memorable night out. It has gained a reputation for its bar and club scene, and this is not only because of the availability of strip clubs suitable for those on a stag weekend. Whether you're after cultural experiences, quality beer, DJs or anything in between, there will be plenty to keep you entertained.

The selection of discos and dance clubs available is much more extensive than it used to be, and when it comes to nighttime activities, there is an abundance of options. It is recommended to plan ahead for a big night out. Prices in the city's drinking venues can also vary greatly, from swanky bars that have a high cost to more affordable pubs and cellars. The Old Town area has some beautiful bars, with rooftop bars offering cocktails to darker and more atmospheric basements.

It is still possible to find lap-dancing clubs in Prague, however many venues in and around Old Town have either banned or strongly discouraged stag parties, so it is not the same destination as it used to be for a budget night out.

The Czechs are renowned for their beer and music, and it is a great way to spend an evening in Prague – enjoying top-notch lagers in a friendly bar or beer hall with the locals. Music fans can then move on to a unique and dynamic music club, such as a jazz club.

BARS IN PRAGUE

<u>Hemingway Bar</u>

This bar is dedicated to Ernest Hemingway's favorite drinks: absinthe, rum, and champagne. It offers over 200 varieties of rum and the most extensive selection of absinthe in the Czech Republic. This is the spot for anyone who loves a great cocktail.

Address: It is located in Staré Město (Old Town) at Karolíny Světlé 26, Prague 1, 110 00

Telephone: +420 773 974 764

Website: http://www.hemingwaybar.cz/bar-prague.

Pivovarsky Klub

Pivovarsky Klub is the place to go to experience the Czech Republic's passion for beer. With more than 200 bottled beers and six on tap at a time, you can sample traditional Czech beer as well as brews from Belgium, Germany and beyond. Plus, you can enjoy great food to pair with your beverages.

Address: It's located in Karlín at Křižíkova 17, Prague 8, 180 00

Telephone: +420 2223 15777

Website: http://www.pivovarskyklub.com/?lang=en.

u Zlatého tygra (Golden Tiger)

u Zlatého tygra (Golden Tiger) is a classic tavern that serves up a variety of traditional pilsner, local pork dishes and coffee. Despite being located in a touristy part of the Old Town; it remains popular with locals. It even hosted former president Václav Havel and Bill Clinton.

Address: Husova 228/17, Prague 1, 110 00

Telephone: +420 2222 21111

Website: http://www.uzlatehotygra.cz/en.

CLUBS IN PRAGUE

Duplex Club

For clubs, Duplex Club is a great option. Located on Wenceslas Square, it has a rooftop terrace during the day and a swanky lounge bar at night. It's often filled with Prague's top DJs and chic crowd, and it even hosted Mick Jagger's 60th birthday!

Address: Nové Město (New Town) at Václavské námestí 21, Prague, 110 00

Telephone: +420 7322 21111

website: http://www.duplex.cz/duplex-events/duplex-sunset-sessions.

Fashion Club

Fashion Club has been a hit ever since it opened, aiming to draw Prague's most attractive people with its fast service, stylish cocktails, and top-notch DJs. Located on the rooftop of a former Communist department store, the venue features a chic, contemporary atmosphere aimed at the young and affluent. Aside from its appealing aesthetics, the club boasts a fantastic view and an exquisite in-house restaurant.

Address: Located at Náměstí Republiky 8, Prague, 110 00

Telephone: +420 224 815 733

Website: http://www.f-club.cz/en

M1 Lounge Bar & Club

M1 Lounge Bar & Club is an important contributor to Prague's nightlife, owned by an expat from New York. It's luxurious atmosphere is enhanced by an expansive dance floor, a cocktail bar, and exclusive VIP spaces. Music is an integral part of the experience, with the club's expert DJs spinning a selection of hip-hop and house, R&B and indie rock.

Address: Located at Staré Město (Old Town), Masná 1, Prague 1, 110 00

Telephone: +420 2271 95235

Website: http://www.m1lounge.com

LIVE MUSIC IN PRAGUE

MeetFactory

MeetFactory is an excellent spot to enjoy live music, operating as an art gallery and theatre during the day and a venue for regional artists and upcoming bands at night, playing a range of alternative, rock and folk tunes.

Address: Located at Ke Sklárně 3213/15, Prague 5, 150 00

Telephone: +420 251 551 796

Website: http://www.meetfactory.cz/en/

Palác Akropolis

Palác Akropolis is a well known cultural complex, hosting around one thousand events a year ranging from art, music, and theatre. Despite its large size, it retains an intimate atmosphere where you can find both local and international indie, rock, and metal artists, such as Marianne Faithful, Megadeth or Sigur Rós. Tickets to shows here tend to fill up quickly, so make sure to reserve yours early to avoid disappointment.

Address: Located at Žižkov, Kubelíkova 1548/27, Prague, 130 00

Telephone: +420 2963 30911

Website: http://www.palacakropolis.com

Reduta Jazz Club

This historic venue, established in the 1950s, is considered to be the oldest and most well-known jazz club in Prague. Over the years, it has welcomed a range of esteemed musicians, including former President of the USA, Bill Clinton, who famously performed on his saxophone here. Live music is performed every night.

Address: Located on the outskirts of Staré Město (Old Town), Národní třída 20, Prague 1, 110 00

Telephone: +420 2249 33487

Website: http://www.redutajazzclub.cz/en

Rudolfinum

This exquisite neo-Renaissance building in the heart of the city has been the home of the Czech Philharmonic Orchestra since 1946. It is a popular tourist destination in its own right and is especially vibrant during Prague's Spring Music Festival. It is fitting that Rudolfinum is the seat of the world-class orchestra, as some of the Czech Republic's most renowned composers, including Antonin Dvorak and Bedrich Smetana, hail from the country.

Address: Located at Josefov, Alšovo nábřeží 12, Prague 1, 110 00

Telephone: +420 227 059 227

Website: http://www.rudolfinum.cz/en

ESSENTIAL PHRASES TO KNOW BEFORE TRAVELING TO CZECH REPUBLIC

The Czech Republic's official language is Czech, which is spoken by 96 percent of the populace. Nevertheless, there is no need to worry; you can communicate effectively using English, particularly in urban areas. Czech is also closely related to the Polish and Slovak languages. In any case, Slovaks and Czechs usually converse without any difficulty.

Worldwide, there are 10 million Czech speakers, most of whom are located in the Czech Republic. Since it is a Slavic language, Czech is closely connected to Slovak, which is spoken in the neighboring country, Slovakia. Although it is based on the Cyrillic script, the Czech language still uses the Latin alphabet instead of the Cyrillic one. It successfully transmits the sound by incorporating diacritics and various other symbols, thereby adapting it to the Czech language.

For many people, Czech is the perfect Slavic language to learn. This is because it uses the Latin alphabet and the phoneme writing system (where each character stands for one sound) is relatively straightforward. Nevertheless, certain elements may still be challenging, but learning Czech is an incredibly rewarding experience, and it can open the doors to learning other languages that are closely related to it. Regardless of why you are learning basic phrases in Czech, you will derive a certain degree of pleasure from it.

Greetings:

Ahoj (ah-hoy) - Hello

Dobrý den (doh-bree dehn) - Good day

Dobré ráno   (dob-reh ra-noh) - Good morning

Dobrý večer (dob-ree ver-chair) - Good evening

Dobrou noc (doh-brah nohts) - Good night

Nazdárek (nahz-dah-rek) - Hi (informal)

Words & Phrases:

Ano (ah-noh) - Yes

Ne (neh) - No

Mluvíte anglicky (mluh-vee-teh ahn-gleets-kee) - Do you speak English

Promiňte (proh-meen-teh) - Excuse me

Omlouvám se (ohm-loh-vahm seh) - Sorry

Prosím (proh-seem) - Please

Děkuji (deh-koo-yee) - Thank you

Pomoc (poh-mots) - Help

Můžete mi pomoct? (moo-zheh-teh mee poh-mohts) - Can you help me?

Questions:

Kde je (kdeh yeh) - Where is....

Kolik to stojí? (koh-lik toh stoh-yee) - How much does it cost?

Kde mohu koupit (kdeh moh-hoo koh-peet) - Where can I buy

Kde je nejbližší bankomat? (kdeh yeh ney-blee-zheesh ee bahn-koh-maht) - Where is the nearest ATM?

Můžete mi poradit? (moo-zheh-teh mee poh-rah-deet) - Can you advise me?

Eating Out:

Chci objednat (kh-chee ohb-jehd-naht) - I would like to order

Máte menu v angličtině? (mah-teh meh-noo v ahn-gleets-tee-neh) - Do you have a menu in English

Můžete mi doporučit něco? (moo-zheh-teh mee doh-poh-roo-cheet neh-tsoh) - Can you recommend something?

Máte otevřeno? (mah-teh oh-teh-vrezh-eh-noh) - Is it open?

Můžete mi přinést účet? (moo-zheh-teh mee preen-nehst oo-chet) - Can I have the bill please?

Getting Around:

Kolik je to odtud? (koh-lik yeh toh ohd-tuhd) - How far is it from here?

Mohu jet autobusem? (moh-hoo yeht oh-toh-boo-sehm) - Can I go by bus?

Kde je nádraží? (kdeh yeh nah-drah-zhee) - Where is the train station?

Mohu jet letadlem? (moh-hoo yeht leh-tahd-lehm) - Can I go by plane?

Numbers:

Jedna (yehd-nah) - One

Dva (dvah) - Two

Tři (treh) - Three

Čtyři (chti-ree) - Four

Pět (peht) - Five

Šest (shehst) - Six

Sedm (sehdm) - Seven

Osm (ohsm) - Eight

Devět (deh-vet) - Nine

Deset (deh-seht) – Ten

THE PERFECT PRAGUE ITINERARY FOR 5 DAYS

S pending five days in Prague is an ideal way to experience all the beauty and grandeur the city has to offer. To make the most of your stay, I've put together a comprehensive five-day guide so you can visit the best attractions and towns in the area.

DAY 1: EXPLORE PRAGUE CASTLE AND MALÁ STRANA QUARTER

Start your Prague exploration by visiting the iconic Prague Castle complex. To avoid long queues, it is recommended to buy tickets in advance or book a guided tour. Inside the walls you will find various historical monuments such as St. George's Basilica and Convent, St. Vitus Cathedral, the former Royal Palace and the Golden Alley. Once done, you can wander around the neighbourhood and admire the beautiful medieval mansions and houses.

Opening hours: From November to March, 9am - 4pm; from April to October, 9am - 5pm

Entry fee: Approximately €16 per person

Duration of visit: 2 - 3 hours

Spend The Afternoon Exploring Mala Strana.

Treat yourself to a delicious lunch in one of the many restaurants located in the Castle Quarter. Afterwards, embark on a walking tour to discover some of the oldest attractions that Mala Strana has to offer. With its vast historical and cultural significance, this area is not too big to wander around, so make sure to check out the must-see spots.

- Start by visiting the small town square, a favourite meeting place since its inception.
- Next, take a stroll around Kampa Island, Prague's most beautiful and popular garden area.
- Don't forget to pay a visit to John Lennon's Wall, a work of art that served as a symbol of resistance against the Soviet regime in Czechoslovakia.
- To end the day, head to Petrin Hill and marvel at the spectacular views from the top of the Petrin Tower.

- You will also find two of the area's most iconic religious monuments - the Church of Our Lady of Victory and the Church of St. Nicholas - nearby.

DAY 2: EXPLORE THE OLDEST PARTS OF PRAGUE.

Devote your second day to exploring the older neighbourhoods on the east side of the river, including Staré Město and Josefov.

Start your morning with a tour of the Jewish Quarter to learn about its history and appreciate its culture. Make sure to visit the Old Jewish Cemetery and the six synagogues.

Opening hours: Note that the cemetery is open from 9am-4.30pm (November-March) and until 6pm (April-October)

Entrance fee: Approximately €4.5. It is also closed on Saturdays.

Duration: Allow two to three hours for the tour.

Experience The Best of Staré Město (Old Town)

To truly experience the best of Staré Město, a visit to Prague would not be complete without a tour of the city's Old Town. While exploring the area you can appreciate the exquisite architecture and take a stroll on the renowned Kaprova street. A few must-see landmarks of the Old Town are: The Clementinum, the Prague National Library and the Astronomical Tower.

Clementinum

Opening hours: The Clementinum is open from 10am to 5pm on Sunday to Thursday and from 10am to 5.30pm on Fridays and Saturdays.

Admission fee: An adult ticket is approximately €13.

Duration: You should plan to spend an hour in the exhibition area.

Old Town Square and Surroundings

A short 8-minute walk from the Clementinum will take you to the Old Town Square with the Old Town Hall, Astronomical Clock Tower and the Church of Our Lady before Týn.

Church of Our Lady before Týn.

Sunset at The Powder Tower

For a breathtaking view of the city, you should visit the Powder Tower before sunset.

Opening hours: The Powder Tower is open from 10:00-18:00 (November to February); 10:00-20:00 (March and October) and 10:00-22:00 (April-September).

Entrance fee: Approximately €9.50 per person.

Relaxing Evening Filled with Tapas and Beers

After a day of exploring the streets and monuments, why not indulge in a relaxing evening filled with tasty tapas and flavorful beers. Sample some of the best Czech craft beers in the world at any of these traditional pubs located near Staré Město:

- U Zlateho Tygra or The Tiger of Oroc in Husova 228/17
- Krcma in Kostecna 925/4
- Lokal Dlouhaaa in Dlouha 731/33
- U Parlamentu in Valentinska 52/8.

DAY 3: VISIT A NAZI CONCENTRATION CAMP.

On the third day of your journey, visit the Terezin Concentration Camp, located in the outskirts of Prague. You can walk along the Charles Bridge, appreciating its impressive sculptures. This concentration camp was established in 1941 and was used as a transit camp for those who were sent to extermination centres in Poland and Belarus.

The poor conditions and forced labour were designed to kill the elderly and weak Czech Jews before they arrived to their final destination. If you wish to witness this dark chapter in Czechoslovakian history, several companies offer tours to the Terezin Ghetto, with an approximate cost of €55 per person.

Opens: In the morning.

Duration: 5 hours.

Make Your Way to The Charles Bridge Before Sunset

Before you finish your tour of the Terezin concentration camp, make sure you have ample time to check out some of the monuments that might have been missed in the preceding days. In the late afternoon, why not make your way to the Charles Bridge, and take a stroll across it while watching the sun set over the Vltava River?

The oldest and most picturesque pedestrian bridge in Prague, the Charles Bridge connects two of the most visited areas of the city - Staré Město and Mala Strana. Every day, tourists flock to the bridge to marvel at its 30 statues, particularly the Statue of Saint Nepomuk, which is believed to grant wishes. With its breathtaking views, don't forget to bring your camera with you!

Statue of Saint Nepomuk

Take the Prague Ghost Tour

Take the Prague Ghost Tour for an unforgettable evening: explore the impressive Czech gothic buildings illuminated by night lighting, accompanied by spine-chilling stories about local beliefs and legends. Be sure to book in advance as these tours fill up quickly and are offered in English. Stops on the tour include walking through the old alleys of the Jewish quarter, visiting small churches, convents and medieval houses.

Duration: The tour generally begins after sunset and lasts roughly two hours

Price: Starting at €19 per person.

DAY 4: GET ACQUAINTED WITH NOVÉ MĚSTO (NEW TOWN)

You will have the chance to get acquainted with Nové Město, the contemporary part of Prague. Start your day off by discovering Wenceslas Square, the iconic destination that has been the epicenter of many revolutions and protests throughout Prague's modern history. There are a variety of retail stores and eateries that you can explore here.

Wenceslas Square

Afterwards, make your way to the National Museum of Prague. This museum is the largest in the city and boasts a great collection of zoological specimens, making it a great place for families to visit. Be sure to take some time to admire the Renaissance facade and interiors of the museum.

Opening hours: The museum is open daily from 10am to 6pm

Admission: Approximately €10.

Duration: Allow yourself two hours to explore the museum and its most interesting works.

National Museum of Prague

Grand Hotel Europa

Before concluding your sightseeing around Wenceslas Square, make sure to take in the stunning Art Nouveau façade of Grand Hotel Europa. Don't forget to take some pictures before heading to the Nové Město district.

Take A Trip to The Vyšehrad District

In the afternoon, take a trip to the Vyšehrad district. You can get there by tram, metro or even a taxi but I recommend travelling by tram. From the Václavské náměstí station, take line 14 and alight at Ostrčilovo náměstí station. At the top of a hill, the fortress offers a breathtaking view of the river and the city. Inside, you can explore the Vyšehrad Gallery, St. Martin's Rotunda, the underground corridors and the Brick Gate.

Opening hours: From 10am to 5pm from November to March and from 10am to 6pm from April to October.

Entrance fee: Around 5€.

Spend A Memorable Evening Aboard a Boat On the Vltava River.

Enjoy a delightful dinner accompanied by live music and stunning views of Prague at sunset. As dusk approaches, the iconic buildings are bathed in a magical golden glow. You can also opt for the Jazz Boat tour, where the musicians perform wonderful jazz songs throughout the cruise.

Meeting time: For dinner at the designated spot.

Price: Starting from €60.

Duration: Book at least three hours for this excursion.

DAY 5: RELAX AND UNWIND IN THE CZECH SPAS.

On your last day in Prague, venture outside and savour the beauty and restorative effects of the Czech spas, renowned for their stunning scenery and therapeutic effects.

Karlovy Vary Spa Trip

A trip to the Karlovy Vary region, renowned for its spas and remarkable Baroque architecture, is one of the most popular excursions from Prague. Founded by Emperor Charles IV, according to local legend, it was while chasing a deer that the emperor first discovered the area's thermal springs.

There are many ways to get to the Karlovy Vary region, but the most convenient way is to book an excursion from Prague. Excursion buses usually depart from the city centre, and the itinerary may vary depending on the company you hire. However, the usual sites of interest include: the twelve spas in Karlovy, the historic architecture of Marianske Lazne, and the Renaissance columns in Karlovy.

Time: Excursions to Karlovy Vary usually leave from Stare Mesto at around 9am.

Price: Typically cost approximately €100.

Duration: The excursion, including transfers to and from the Karlovy Vary region, will take around 10 hours, so it is best to plan for a full day.

The Czech Republic offers plenty of amazing places to visit, and a trip to Prague with its environs is sure to leave you with lasting memories.

Karlovy Vary

Hope you enjoyed your read.

Please kindly leave a review.

....

YOU MAY ALSO ENJOY OTHER BOOKS FROM THE AUTHOR:

QATAR TRAVEL GUIDE 2022: 40+ Ultimate Qatar Experiences (With Pictures), Your Guide to All You Need to Know, where to Go, what to See, what to Do and Local Tips.

DUBAI, UAE TRAVEL GUIDE: 70+ Ultimate Dubai Experiences (With Pictures), Your Guide to All You Need to Know, where to Go, what to Do and Local Tips. (Middle Eastern Travel Guide)

Printed in Great Britain
by Amazon